Solar Power

Andrea Rivera

abdopublishing.com

Published by Abdo Zoom™, PO Box 398166, Minneapolis, Minnesota 55439. Copyright © 2017 by Abdo Consulting Group, Inc. International copyrights reserved in all countries. No part of this book may be reproduced in any form without written permission from the publisher. Abdo Zoom™ is a trademark and logo of Abdo Consulting Group, Inc.

Printed in the United States of America, North Mankato, Minnesota
102016
012017

THIS BOOK CONTAINS
RECYCLED MATERIALS

Cover Photo: Filip Fuxa/Shutterstock Images
Interior Photos: Filip Fuxa/Shutterstock Images, 1 ; Iakov Kalinin/Shutterstock Images, 4–5; Gyuszko Photo/Shutterstock Images, 5; Frederico Rostagno/Shutterstock Images, 6; Shutterstock Images, 7, 12, 13, 21; Tom Grundy/Shutterstock Images, 8; Jens Meyer/AP Images, 9; iStockphoto, 10–11, 16–17; Alfons Hauke/imageBROKER/Alamy, 15; Dmitriy Raykin/Shutterstock Images, 18; Olivier Le Queinec/Shutterstock Images, 19

Editor: Emily Temple
Series Designer: Madeline Berger
Art Direction: Dorothy Toth

Publisher's Cataloging-in-Publication Data
Names: Rivera, Andrea, author.
Title: Solar power / by Andrea Rivera.
Description: Minneapolis, MN : Abdo Zoom, 2017. | Series: Our renewable Earth | Includes bibliographical references and index.
Identifiers: LCCN 2016948927 | ISBN 9781680799415 (lib. bdg.) | ISBN 9781624025273 (ebook) | ISBN 9781624025839 (Read-to-me ebook)
Subjects: LCSH: Solar energy--Juvenile literature. | Renewable energy sources--Juvenile literature.
Classification: DDC 333.792/3--dc23
LC record available at http://lccn.loc.gov/2016948927

Table of Contents

The sun is a star. It gives off energy. The energy comes to Earth as light and heat.

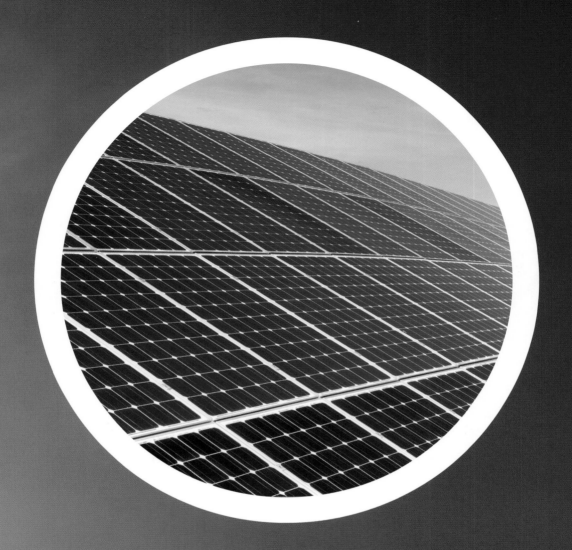

It is turned into **electricity**.
This is solar power.

Technology

Solar panels collect sunlight. They have glass covers.

The glass has a coating.
The coating helps soak up light.

Engineering

Some solar power systems have curved mirrors.

They send light into tubes.
It heats oil inside the tubes.

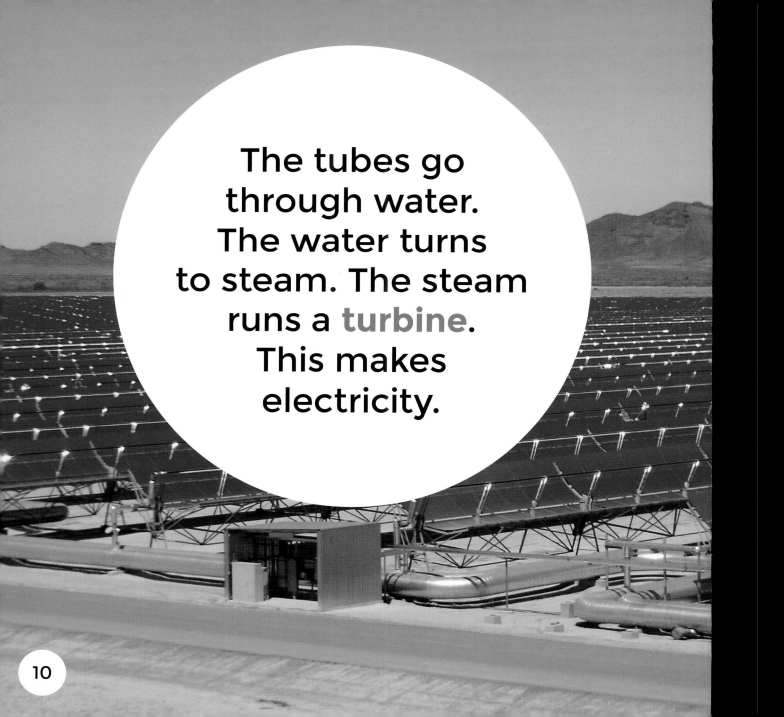

The tubes go through water. The water turns to steam. The steam runs a **turbine**. This makes electricity.

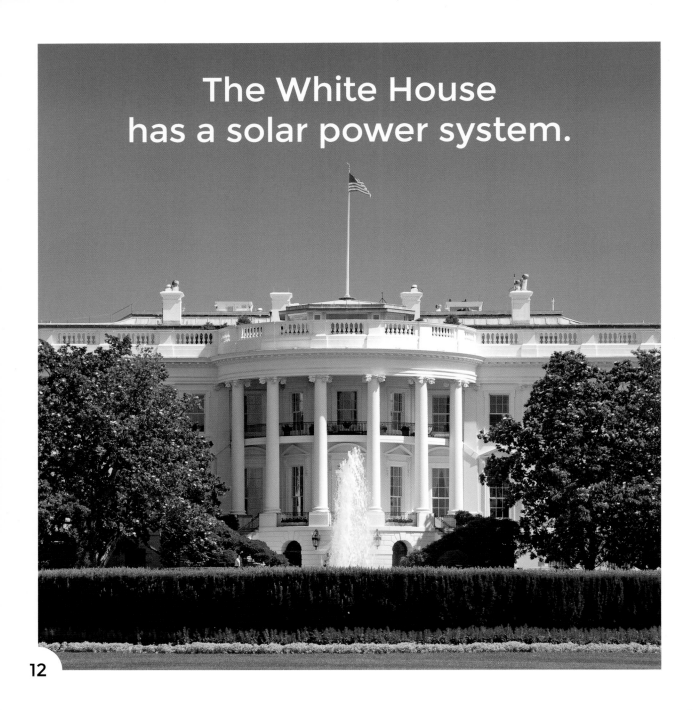

The White House
has a solar power system.

President Barack Obama had it put on the roof. The system heats the water inside the house.

13

Art

Some sculptures use solar power. One artist made giant flowers. Solar panels are on top. They soak in light. The panels power lights on the flowers.

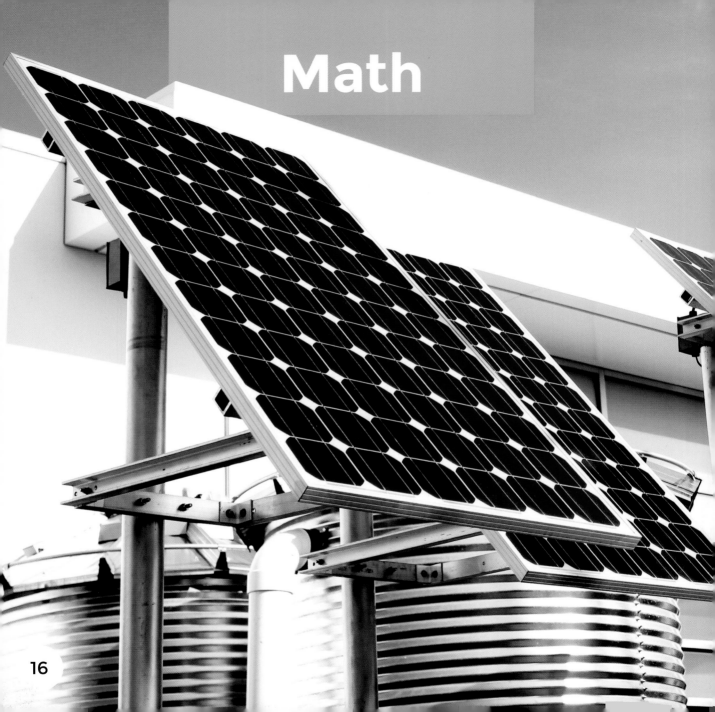

Math

Electricity is measured in watts. One solar panel can create 200 watts of electricity.

Some lightbulbs need 10 watts.

Lighting 20 lightbulbs takes 200 watts. One solar panel can power 20 lightbulbs.

- More than one million homes in the United States have solar panels.

- About 1 percent of the world's electricity comes from solar energy.

- The largest solar power plant in the United States is in Nevada. It has more than 70,000 panels.

- Germany uses more solar power than any other country.

Glossary

electricity - a form of energy that can be carried through wires and power things such as machines and lights.

sculpture - an art form that is 3-D (not flat), like a statue.

solar panel - a flat surface covered with a material that collects energy from the sun.

turbine - an engine that includes blades. Air, steam, or water moves the blades.

Booklinks

For more information
on solar power, please visit
booklinks.abdopublishing.com

 In on STEAM!

Learn even more with the Abdo Zoom
STEAM database. Check out
abdozoom.com for more information.

Index